A

From the Editor

"If you want to lift yourself up,
lift up someone else."

—Booker T. Washington

Research has shown that the old adage "It's better to give than to receive" is true after all. The positive feelings we experience when helping others is the greatest feeling in the world. It gives us a sense of purpose and makes us feel happier and more satisfied about life in general.

In most of our communities, we all have friends and neighbors who are dealing with stress of some kind, be it cancer, Alzheimer's, single parents, moving loved ones into a nursing home or premature babies.

With careful thought, we have created this special book, *Caring Crochet*, to add a touch of beauty and comfort to the lives of others less fortunate.

In sharing our time and talents with others by small acts of kindness, the rewards will be many for everyone involved.

Happy stitching,

Connie Ellison

Simple Shawl

Design by Michele Maks

Skill Level

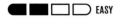 EASY

Finished Measurements

19 inches wide x 60 inches long

Materials

- Berroco Comfort medium (worsted) weight nylon/acrylic yarn (3½ oz/210 yds/100g per skein):
  4 skeins #9838 raspberry tart
- Size J/10/6mm crochet hook or size needed to obtain gauge
- Tapestry needle

Gauge

10 sts = 4 inches

Pattern Notes

Weave in loose ends as work progresses.

Chain-4 at beginning of row counts as a treble crochet unless otherwise stated.

Join with slip stitch as indicated unless otherwise stated.

Shawl

Body

Row 1 (RS): Ch 51, sc in 2nd ch from hook, sc in each rem ch across, turn. *(50 sc)*

Row 2: Ch 4 *(see Pattern Notes)*, tr in each sc across, turn. *(50 tr)*

Row 3: Ch 1, sc in each tr across, turn.

Rows 4–13: [Rep rows 2 and 3 alternately] 5 times. At end of last row, fasten off.

Row 14: Join yarn in first sc of last row, ch 1, sc in same sc as beg ch-1, sc in each sc across, turn.

Rows 15–26: [Rep rows 2 and 3 alternately] 6 times. At end of next row, do not turn.

Row 27: Rep row 14.

Rows 28–39: [Rep rows 2 and 3 alternately] 6 times. At end of last row, do not turn.

Row 40: Rep row 14.

Rows 41–52: [Rep rows 2 and 3 alternately] 6 times. At end of last row, do not turn.

Rows 53–65: Rep rows 14–26.

Rows 66–78: Rep rows 27–39.

Rows 79–91: Rep rows 40–52.

Border

Rnd 1: Working around outer edge, 3 sc in corner st, sc evenly sp around, working 3 sc in each rem corner, **join** *(see Pattern Notes)* in beg sc. Fasten off. ●

Autumn to Winter Hat

Design by Katherine Eng

Skill Level

 INTERMEDIATE

Finished Size

One size fits most

Materials

- Berroco Comfort Chunky bulky (chunky) weight nylon/acrylic yarn (3½ oz/150 yds/100g per skein):
  2 skeins #5703 barley
- Size I/9/5.5mm crochet hook or size needed to obtain gauge
- Tapestry needle
- ⅜-inch-long decorative metal beads: 13

Gauge

Rows 1–3 = 1½ inches x 6 inches

Pattern Notes

Weave in loose ends as work progresses.

To make smaller Hat, use smaller hook.

Join with slip stitch as indicated unless otherwise stated.

Chain-4 at beginning of round counts as a double crochet and chain-1 unless otherwise stated.

Hat

Row 1: Ch 18, sc in 2nd ch from hook and in each rem ch across, turn. *(17 sc)*

Row 2: Ch 1, sc in **back lp** *(see Stitch Guide)* of each of first 5 sts, sc in **front lp** *(see Stitch Guide)* in each of next 12 sts *(top edge)*, turn.

Row 3: Ch 1, sc in front lp of each of first 12 sts, sc in back lp of each of last 5 sts, turn.

Rows 4–49: [Rep rows 2 and 3 alternately] 23 times.

Row 50: Rep row 2. At end of row, leaving 12-inch end, fasten off.

Assembly

Working in back lps, sew row 1 and row 50 tog, forming tube.

Top

Rnd 1: Now working in rnds, with seam at back, join with sc in end of first row at top edge, sc in end of each row around, **join** *(see Pattern Notes)* in beg sc. *(50 sc)*

Rnd 2: Ch 1, working in front lps, sc in each st around, join in beg sc.

Rnd 3: Ch 1, sc in same st as beg ch-1, ch 1, sk next st, [sc in next st, ch 1, sk next st] around, join in beg sc.

Rnd 4: Sl st in next ch-1 sp, ch 1, sc in same sp as beg ch-1, sc in each rem ch-1 sp around, join in beg sc. *(25 sc)*

Rnd 5: Ch 4 *(see Pattern Notes)*, [dc in next st, ch 1, sk next st] around, join in 3rd ch of beg ch-4.

Rnd 6: Sl st in next ch-1 sp, ch 8, sl st in same sp as beg ch-8, (sl st, ch 8, sl st) in each ch-1 sp around, join in beg sl st. Fasten off.

Tie

Leaving 6-inch end, ch 70. Leaving 6-inch end, fasten off.

Weave Tie under and over sts of rnd 5, beg and ending in back.

Pull to tighten and close center top. Tie in bow.

Thread 6 beads onto 1 end of Tie and 7 beads onto other end of Tie. Tie knot in each end to secure beads. Separate strands below knot and trim ends. ●

Cheery Tissue Box Cover

Design by Jennine Korejko

Skill Level

 EASY

Finished Measurements

5 inches wide x 5 inches long x 6 inches tall

Materials

- Berroco Comfort medium (worsted) weight nylon/acrylic yarn (3½ oz/210 yds/100g per skein):
  - 1 oz each #9785 falseberry heather and #9701 ivory
  - 2 yds each 5 scrap colors
- Size I/9/5.5mm crochet hook or size needed to obtain gauge
- Tapestry needle

Gauge

Rnds 1 and 2 = 1½ inches high

Pattern Notes

Weave in loose ends as work progresses.

Join with slip stitch as indicated unless otherwise stated.

Chain-3 at beginning of round counts as a double crochet unless otherwise stated.

Special Stitch

Puff stitch (puff st): [Yo, insert hook in st indicated, yo, draw up lp] twice, yo and draw through all 5 lps on hook.

Cover

Side Square

Make 4.

Rnd 1 (RS): With any scrap color, ch 4, **join** (see Pattern Notes) in first ch to form ring, **ch 3** (see Pattern Notes), 15 dc in ring, join in 3rd ch of beg ch-3. Fasten off. (16 dc)

Rnd 2: Join scrap color in same ch as joining, ch 3, dc in same ch as beg ch-3, ch 2, (2 dc, ch 3, 2 dc) in same ch as beg ch-3 (beg corner made), ch 2, 2 dc in same ch-3 as beg ch-3, **change color** (see Stitch Guide) to next scrap color in last dc, sk next 3 dc, *2 dc in next dc, ch 2, (2 dc, ch 3, 2 dc) in same dc (corner made), ch 2, 2 dc in same dc, change color to next scrap color in last dc, sk next 3 dc, rep from * twice, join in 3rd ch of beg ch-3. Fasten off. (32 dc)

Rnd 3: Join ivory in ch-3 sp of any corner, ch 1, (2 sc, ch 2, 2 sc) in same sp as beg ch-1 (sc corner made), 2 sc in next ch-2 sp, ch 1, dc in sp between next two 2-dc groups, ch 1, 2 sc in next ch-2 sp, *(2 sc , ch 2, 2 sc) in next corner ch-3 sp (sc corner made), 2 sc in next ch-2 sp, ch 1, dc in sp between next two 2-dc groups, ch 1, 2 sc in next ch-2 sp, rep from * twice, join in first sc.

Rnd 4: Ch 3, dc in next sc, (dc, ch 2, dc) in next corner ch-2 sp (dc corner made), dc in each of next 4 sc, in next ch-1 sp, in next dc and in next ch-1 sp, *dc in each of next 4 sc, (dc, ch 2, dc) in next corner ch-2 sp (dc corner made), dc in each of next 4 sc, in next ch-1 sp, in next dc and in next ch-1 sp, rep from * twice, dc in each of next 2 sc, join in 3rd ch of beg ch-3. Fasten off. (52 dc)

Rnd 5: Hold piece with WS facing you; join ivory in same ch as joining of previous rnd, ch 1, sc in same ch as beg ch-1, [**puff st** *(see Special Stitch)* in next dc, sc in next dc] 3 times, in next corner ch-2 sp work (puff st, ch 2, puff st), *sc in next dc, [puff st in next dc, sc in next dc] 6 times, (puff st, ch 2, puff st) in next corner ch-2 sp, rep from * twice, sc in next dc, puff st in last dc, join in first sc. Fasten off.

Top Square

Rnd 1 (RS): With scrap color, ch 16, join in first ch to form ring, ch 1, working in **back lp** *(see Stitch Guide)*, sc in same ch as joining and in each rem ch around, join in first sc. Fasten off. *(16 sc)*

Rnd 2: Join scrap color in same sc as joining, ch 3, dc in same sc as beg ch-3, ch 2, (2 dc, ch 3, 2 dc) in same sc *(beg corner made)*, ch 2, dc in same sc, change color to next scrap color in last dc, sk next 3 sc, *2 dc in next sc, ch 2, (2 dc, ch 3, 2 dc) in same sc *(corner made)*, ch 2, 2 dc in same sc, change color to next scrap color in last dc, sk next 3 sc, rep from * twice, join in 3rd ch of beg ch-3. Fasten off.

Rnds 3–5: Rep rnds 3–5 of Side Square.

Assembly

Hold 2 Side Squares with WS tog and carefully match sts. With tapestry needle and falseberry heather, and beg and ending in corner sps, sew sides tog along 1 edge. In same manner, sew rem Side Squares tog and sew Top Square to top edges of Side Squares.

Bottom Edging

Rnd 1 (RS): Hold piece with RS facing, join falseberry heather in any st, ch 1, sc in same st, in each rem st and in each corner sp, join in first sc. Fasten off.

Rnd 2 (WS): Hold piece with WS facing you; join ivory in same sc as joining of previous rnd, ch 1, sc in same sc as beg ch-1, puff st in next sc, *sc in next sc, puff st in next sc, rep from * around, join in first sc, **turn.**

Rnd 3 (RS): Ch 1, sc in same sc as beg ch-1, sc in each rem sc around, join in first sc. Fasten off. ●

Chevron Band Slippers

Design by Rebecca Huber

Skill Level

Finished Sizes

Instructions given fit woman's size small; changes for medium and large are in [ ].

Finished Measurement

7–7½ [8–8½, 9–9½] inches long

Materials

- Berroco Comfort medium (worsted) weight nylon/acrylic yarn (3½ oz/210 yds/100g per skein):
  - 1 skein #9763 navy blue
- Berroco Comfort DK light (DK) weight nylon/acrylic yarn (1¾ oz/178 yds/50g per skein):
  - 1 skein each #2703 barley, #2733 turquoise, #2700 chalk and #2763 navy blue
- Sizes G/6/4mm and H/8/5mm crochet hooks or sizes needed to obtain gauge
- Tapestry needle
- Stitch markers: 2

Gauge

Size G hook and worsted yarn: 5 sts = 1 inch

Size H hook and DK yarn: 9 sts = 2 inches

Take time to check gauge.

Pattern Notes

Work Sole with worsted-weight yarn. Work rest of Slipper with DK-weight yarn as indicated.

Work in continuous rounds; do not turn or join unless otherwise stated.

Mark first stitch of round. Move marker as work progresses.

When working in rows across Chevron Top of Toe, work in stitches of each row and in stitches on last round of Toe.

Join with slip stitch as indicated unless otherwise stated.

Special Stitch

Long single crochet (long sc): Insert hook in indicated st or sp, yo, pull up lp to height of current rnd, yo, pull through all lps on hook.

Slipper

Make 2.

Sole

Rnd 1: With size G hook and **blue** *(see Pattern Notes)*, ch 23 [27, 31], 2 sc in 2nd ch from hook, sc in each of next 12 [14, 16] chs, hdc in next ch, dc in each of next 7 [9, 11] chs, 7 dc in last ch *(toe)*, **place marker** *(see Pattern Notes)* in 4th dc of last 7 dc, working along opposite side of beg ch, dc in each of next 7 [9, 11] chs, hdc in next ch, sc in each of next 12 [14, 16] chs, 2 sc in last ch. *(51 [59, 67] sts)*

Rnd 2: Sc in next st, 2 sc in next st, sc in each of next 14 [16, 18] sts, hdc in next st, dc in each of next 7 [9, 11] sts, 2 dc in next st, 3 dc in next st, 2 dc in next st, dc in each of next 7 [9, 11] sts, hdc in next st, sc in each of next 14 [16, 18] sts, 2 sc in next st, sc in last st. *(57 [65, 73] sts)*

Rnd 3: Sc in next st, 2 sc in next st, sc in each of next 25 [29, 33] sts, 2 sc in next st, 3 sc in next st, 2 sc in next st, sc in each of next 25 [29, 33] sts, 2 sc in next st, sc in last st. *(63 [71, 79] sts)*

Rnd 4: Sc in next sc, 2 sc in each of next 2 sc, sc in each of next 26 [30, 34] sc, 2 sc in next sc, sc in next sc, 3 sc in next sc, sc in next sc, 2 sc in next sc, sc in each of next 26 [30, 34] sc, 2 sc in each of next 2 sc, sc in last sc. *(71 [79, 87] sc)*

Rnd 5: Sc in next sc, 2 sc in next sc, sc in each of next 31 [35, 39] sc, 2 sc in next sc, sc in next sc, 3 sc in next sc, sc in next sc, 2 sc in next sc, sc in each of next 31 [35, 39] sc, 2 sc in next sc, sc in last sc. *(77 [85, 93] sc)*

Rnd 6: Sc in each sc around, **change color** *(see Stitch Guide)* to barley in last st. Fasten off blue.

Sides

Rnds 1–4: With size H hook and barley, sc in each sc around. *(77 [85, 93] sc)*

Toe

Rnd 1: Sc in each of next 37 [41, 45] sc, sk next 2 sc, sc in each rem sc around. *(75 [83, 91] sc)*

Rnd 2: Sc in each of next 37 [41, 45] sc, sk next 2 sc, sc in each rem sc around, change to turquoise in last sc. *(73 [81, 89] sc)*

Note: Count sts to ensure there are an even number of sts on each side of Toe marker.

Rnd 3: Sc in each sc around to 6th sc before center Toe st marker, [**long sc** *(see Special Stitch)* in next sc 1 rnd below, sc in each of next 2 sc] 4 times, long sc in next sc 1 rnd below, sc in each rem sc around, change color to chalk in last sc. *(73 [81, 89] sc)*

Rnd 4: Sc in each of next 35 [39, 43] sc, sk next 2 sc, sc in each rem sc around, change color to turquoise in last sc. *(71, [79, 87] sc)*

Rnd 5: Sc in each of next 35 [39, 43] sc, sk next 2 sc, sc in each rem sc around, change color to barley in last st. *(69 [77, 85] sc)*

Rnd 6: Sc in each of next 33 [37, 41] sc, sk next 2 sc, sc in each rem sc around. *(67 [75, 83] sts)*

Rnd 7: Sc in each of next 33 [37, 41] sc, sk next 2 sc, sc in each rem sc around, do not fasten off, secure working lp with marker. *(65 [73, 81] sts)*

Note: Count sts to ensure there are an even number of sts on each side of Toe marker.

Chevron Top of Toe

Row 1: Now **working in rows** *(see Pattern Notes)*, with size H hook, **join** *(see Pattern Notes)* turquoise in 8th [9th, 10th] sc before center Toe marker, sc in each of next 7 [8, 9] sc, sk next 2 sc, sc in each of next 7 [8, 9] sc, sl st in next sc, turn.

Row 2: Ch 1, sc in first sl st, sc in each of next 7 [8, 9] sc, sk next 2 sc, sc in each of next 7 [8, 9] sc, sl st in next sc, turn.

Rows 3 & 4: With chalk, [rep row 2] twice.

Rows 5 & 6: With blue, [rep row 2] twice. At end of last row, fasten off. *(53 [61, 69] sts)*

Edging

Rnd 1: Now working in rnds, pick up lp of barley at back of slipper, **sc dec** *(see Stitch Guide)* in next 2 sc, sc in each of next 16 [19, 23] sc, sc dec in next 2 sc, sc in each of next 6 [7, 8] sc, sk next 2 sc, sc in each of next 6 [7, 8] sc, sc dec in next 2 sc, sc in each of next 17 [20, 22] sc. *(48 [56, 64] sts)*

Rnd 2: Sc in each of next 15 [18, 21] sts, sc dec in next 2 sts, sc in each of next 5 [6, 7] sts, sk next 2 sts, sc in each of next 5 [6, 7] sts, sc dec in next 2 sts, sc in each of next 15 [18, 21] sts, sc dec in last 2 sts. *(43 [51, 59] sts)*

Size Small Only

Rnd 3: Sc in each of next 20 sts, sk next 2 sts, sc in each rem st around. Fasten off. *(41 sts)*

Size Medium Only

Rnd [3]: Sc in each of next 18 sts, sc dec in next 2 sts, sc in each of next 5 sts, sk next 2 sts, sc in each of next 5 sts, sc dec in next 2 sts, sc in each rem st around. Fasten off. *([47] sts)*

Size Large Only

Rnd [3]: Sc dec in next 2 sts, sc in each of next 19 sts, sc dec in next 2 sts, sc in each of next 6 sts, sk next sts, sc in each of next 6 sts, sc dec in next 2 sts, sc in each rem st around. Fasten off. *([54] sts)* ●

Deluxe Lap Robe

Design by Irene Stock

Skill Level

 EASY

Finished Measurements

30 inches wide x 40 inches long

Materials

- Berroco Comfort medium (worsted) weight nylon/ acrylic yarn (3½ oz/210 yds/ 100g per skein): 7 skeins #9834 pot-au-feu
- Size I/9/5.5mm crochet hook or size needed to obtain gauge
- Tapestry needle

Gauge

5 pattern reps = 4 inches; 10 pattern rows = 4 inches

Pattern Notes

Weave in loose ends as work progresses.

Join with slip stitch as indicated unless otherwise stated.

Lap Robe

Body

Row 1: Ch 111, dc in 3rd ch from hook *(beg 2 sk chs count as a ch-2 sp)*, sk next 2 chs, *(sc, ch 2, dc) in next ch, sk next 2 chs, rep from * across to last ch, sc in last ch, turn. *(36 dc, 36 sc, 36 ch-2 sps)*

Row 2: Ch 2, dc in first sc, (sc, ch 2, dc) in each ch-2 sp across to last ch-2 sp, sc in last ch-2 sp, turn.

Rep row 2 until piece measures 40 inches from beg. At end of last row, fasten off.

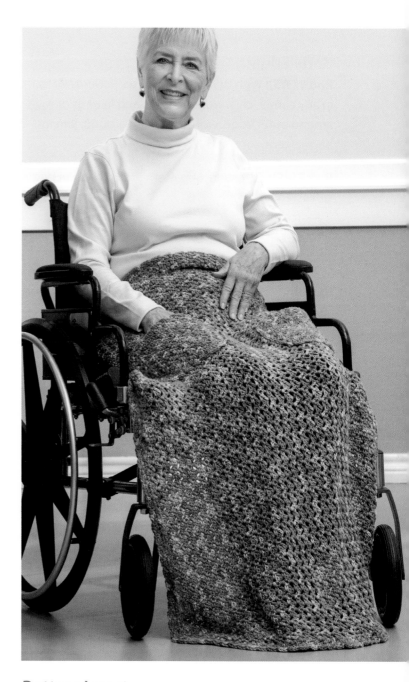

Bottom Insert

Row 1: Ch 36, dc in 3rd ch from hook *(beg 2 sk chs count as a ch-2 sp)*, sk next 2 chs, *(sc, ch 2, dc) in next ch, sk next 2 chs, rep from * across to last ch, sc in last ch, turn. *(8 dc, 8 sc, 8 ch-2 sps)*

Rep row 2 of Body until Insert measures 8½ inches. At end of last row, fasten off.

Center first row of Bottom Insert to first row of Bottom. Bring remainder of first row around sides of Bottom Insert. Pin in place and sew.

Body Edging

Rnd 1 (WS): With WS facing, **join** *(see Pattern Notes)* in any corner, ch 1, working in sts and in ends of rows around outer edge, work in pattern around, join in beg sc, turn.

Rnd 2 (RS): Ch 1, work in pattern around, join in beg sc. Fasten off.

Pocket
Make 2.

Row 1: Ch 36, dc in 3rd ch from hook, sk next 2 chs, *(sc, ch 2, dc) in next ch, sk next 2 chs, rep from * across to last ch, sc in last ch, turn.

Row 2: Ch 2, dc in first sc, (sc, ch 2, dc) in each ch-2 sp across to last ch-2 sp, sc in last ch-2 sp, turn.

Rows 3–12: Rep row 2. At end of last row, fasten off.

Pocket Edging
Rnds 1 & 2: Rep rnds 1 and 2 of Body Edging.

Place Pockets on Body 11 inches from top. Pin in place, centering each Pocket on either side with 6 inches between Pockets. Sew Pockets to Body, leaving tops open.

Tie (Optional)
Make 2.

Ch 101, sl st in 2nd ch from hook, sl st in each rem ch across. Fasten off.

Tie knot in each end.

Fold Tie in half. Pull fold through lp 5 pattern reps from side and 2 rows from top. Pull ends through lp and pull tight. ●

Star Stitch Preemie Blanket

Design by Judy Crow

Skill Level
 EASY

Finished Measurements
22 inches wide x 23 inches long

Gauge
9 star sts = 4 inches; 11 rows in pattern = 4 inches

Materials
- Berroco Comfort DK light (DK) weight nylon/acrylic yarn (1¾ oz/178 yds/50g per skein): 3 skeins #2702 pearl
- Size I/9/5.5mm crochet hook or size needed to obtain gauge
- Tapestry needle

3 LIGHT

Pattern Notes

Double crochet at end of odd-numbered rows is worked in same stitch as last step of star base.

Chain-2 at beginning of each even-numbered row does not count as a stitch.

Join with slip stitch as indicated unless otherwise stated.

Special Stitches

Beginning star stitch (beg star st): Insert hook in 2nd ch from hook, pull up lp, [insert hook in next ch and pull up lp] 4 times, yo and draw through all 6 lps on hook, ch 1 to secure.

Star stitch (star st): Insert hook in ch-1 of last star st, pull up lp, insert hook in side of last lp of last star st and pull up lp, insert hook in st at base of last lp of last star st and pull up lp, [insert hook in next st and pull up lp] twice, yo, draw through all 6 lps on hook, ch 1 to secure.

Blanket

Row 1: Ch 100, **beg star st** *(see Special Stitches)* in 2nd ch from hook and in next 4 chs, ***star st** *(see Special Stitches)* in previous star st and in next 2 chs, rep from * across, **dc in last ch** *(see Pattern Notes)* at base of last lp of last star st, turn. *(48 star sts)*

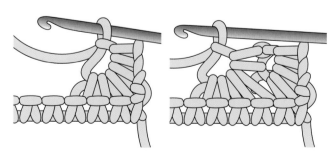

Beginning Star Stitch   **Star Stitch**

Row 2: Ch 2 *(see Pattern Notes)*, *2 hdc in ch-1 of next star st, rep from * across to beg ch-2, hdc in 2nd ch of beg ch-2, turn.

Row 3: Ch 3, beg star st in 2nd and 3rd ch from hook and in first 3 sts, *star st in previous star st and in next 2 sts, rep from * across, dc in last hdc at base of last lp of last star st, turn.

Rows 4–59: [Rep rows 2 and 3 alternately] 28 times.

Row 60: Rep row 2. At end of row, do not fasten off.

Edging

Rnd 1 (RS): Evenly sc around entire blanket, working 3 sc in each corner, **join** *(see Pattern Notes)* in first st.

Rnd 2: Ch 1, **rev sc** *(see Stitch Guide)* in each st around, join in first st. Fasten off. ●

Preemie Cocoon & Hat

Designs by Sue Childress

Skill Level

 INTERMEDIATE

Finished Measurements

Hat: 4 inches tall x 12 inches in circumference

Cocoon: 8 inches long x 13 inches in circumference

Materials

- Berroco Comfort DK light (DK) weight nylon/acrylic yarn (1¾ oz/178 yds/50g per skein):
  1 skein #2850 jump rope
- Size G/6/4mm crochet hook or size needed to obtain gauge
- Tapestry needle
- ⅝-inch-wide ribbon: 18 inches

Gauge

Rnds 1 and 2 = 2 inches

Pattern Notes

Chain-2 at beginning of round counts as first half double crochet unless otherwise stated.

Join with slip stitch as indicated unless otherwise stated.

Slip stitches at beginning of round do not count as stitches unless otherwise stated.

Chain-3 at beginning of round counts as first double crochet unless otherwise stated.

Hat

Rnd 1: Ch 6, sl st in first ch to form ring, **ch 2** (see Pattern Notes), 11 hdc in ring, **join** (see Pattern Notes) in top of beg ch-2. (12 hdc)

Rnd 2: Sl st (see Pattern Notes) in next hdc, **ch 3** (see Pattern Notes), dc in same hdc, 2 dc in each hdc around, join in top of beg ch-3. (24 dc)

Rnd 3: Ch 3, dc in next dc, 2 **fpdc** (see Stitch Guide) around next dc, *dc in each of next 2 dc, 2 fpdc around next dc, rep from * around, join in top of beg ch-3. (16 dc, 16 fpdc)

Rnd 4: Ch 3, dc in each of next 2 sts, 2 fpdc around next st, *dc in each of next 3 sts, 2 fpdc around next st, rep from * around, join in top of beg ch-3. (16 fpdc, 24 dc)

Rnd 5: Ch 3, 2 fpdc around next st, *dc in each of next 4 sts, 2 fpdc around next st, rep from * around to last 3 sts, dc in each of last 3 sts, join in top of beg ch-3. (16 fpdc, 32 dc)

Rnds 6–8: Ch 3, dc in each st around, join in top of beg ch-3. (48 dc)

Rnd 9: Ch 3, **bpdc** (see Stitch Guide) around next st, fpdc around each of next 2 sts, *bpdc around each of next 2 sts, fpdc around each of next 2 sts, rep from * around, join in top of beg ch-3.

Rnds 10 & 11: [Rep rnd 9] twice. Fasten off.

Cocoon

Rnds 1–5: Rep rnds 1–5 for Hat. (48 sts)

Rnd 6: Ch 3, dc in same st, dc in each of next 23 sts, 2 dc in next st, dc in each rem st around, join in top of beg ch-3. (50 sts)

Rnd 7: Ch 3, dc in each of next 3 sts, 2 fpdc around next dc, *dc in each of next 4 dc, 2 fpdc around next dc, rep from * around, join in top of beg ch-3. (40 dc, 20 fpdc)

Rnds 8–11: Ch 3, dc in each of next 4 sts, fpdc around next dc, *dc in each of next 5 sts, fpdc around next st, rep from * around, join in top of beg ch-3.

Rnds 12–17: Ch 3, dc in next st, fpdc around next dc, *dc in each of next 5 sts, fpdc around next st, rep from * around to last 3 sts, dc in each of last 3 sts, join in top of beg ch-3.

Row 18: Now working in rows, sl st in each of next 4 sts, turn, ch 2, **dc dec** (see Stitch Guide) in next 2 sts, *dc in each of next 4 sts, dc dec in next 2 sts, rep from * around to last 3 sts, dc in next st, hdc in next st, turn, leaving last dc unworked. (49 sts)

Row 19: Ch 2, hdc in next st, dc in each rem st across to last 2 sts, hdc in each of last 2 sts, turn.

Row 20: Ch 2, hdc in next st, sk next st, *(dc, hdc) in next st, sk next st, rep from * around to last 2 sts, hdc in each of last 2 sts, turn.

Edging

Rnd 1: Sk first st, sc in each st across last row, evenly sc around opening, join in first sc. Fasten off.

Finishing

Weave in ends. Weave ribbon between sts of row 18 and tie at front of opening. ●

Preemie Cap

Design by Kyleigh C. Hawke

Skill Level

 EASY

Finished Measurement

9 inches in circumference

Materials

- Berroco Comfort DK light (DK) weight nylon/acrylic yarn (1¾ oz/178 yds/50g per skein): 1 skein #2719 sunshine
- Size D/3/3.25mm crochet hook or size needed to obtain gauge
- Tapestry needle

Gauge

5 sc = 1 inch; 6 sc rows = 1 inch

Cap

Row 1: Ch 35, sc in **back lp** (*see Stitch Guide*) of 2nd ch from hook, sc in back lp of each rem ch across, turn. (*34 sc*)

Note: Work all following rows in back lps only.

Row 2: Ch 1, sc in each st across to last 3 sts, leaving last 3 sts unworked, turn. (*31 sc*)

Row 3: Ch 1, sc in each st across, turn.

Row 4: Rep row 2. (*28 sc*)

Row 5: Ch 1, sc in each st across, turn.

Row 6: Ch 1, sc in each st across, [sc in end of row below and next unworked st at same time, sc in each of next 2 unworked sts] twice, turn. (*34 sc*)

Row 7: Ch 1, sc in each st across, turn.

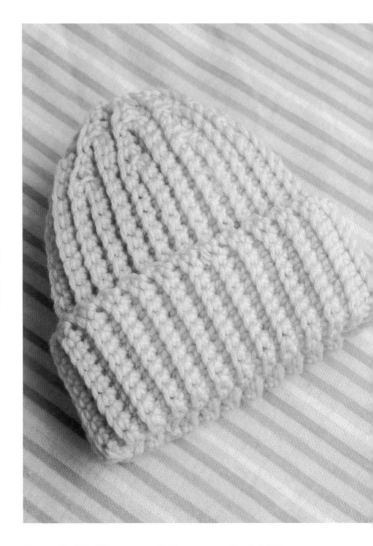

Rows 8–49: [Rep rows 2–7 consecutively] 7 times.

Rows 50–54: Rep rows 2–6. At end of last row, leaving 18-inch end, fasten off.

Finishing

Weave end through ends of rows, pull to gather top of Cap. Sew last and first rows tog and secure end. Weave in ends.

Turn up bottom edge of Cap for cuff as shown in photo. ●

Preemie Booties

Design by Estelle Voelker

Skill Level

 **EASY**

Finished Measurement

Sole: 2½ inches long

Materials
- Berroco Comfort DK light (DK) weight nylon/acrylic yarn (1¾ oz/178 yds/50g per skein):
    1 skein #2719 sunshine
- Size B/1/2.25mm crochet hook or size needed to obtain gauge
- Tapestry needle
- Cord or ¼-inch-wide ribbon: 20 inches

Gauge

6 sc = 1 inch; 4 sc rnds = 1 inch

Pattern Notes

Weave in loose ends as work progresses.

If different-size Booties are desired, use different-size hook and/or yarn weight.

Join with slip stitch as indicated unless otherwise stated.

Chain-2 at beginning of round, if followed by a half double crochet, counts as a half double crochet unless otherwise stated.

Bootie
Make 2.

Sole

Rnd 1: Ch 9, 3 sc in 2nd ch from hook, hdc in each of next 5 chs, dc in next ch, 5 dc in last ch, working on opposite side of foundation ch, dc in next ch, hdc in each of next 5 chs, 2 sc in last ch, **join** *(see Pattern Notes)* in first sc. *(22 sts)*

Rnd 2: Ch 2 *(see Pattern Notes)*, 2 hdc in next st, hdc in each of next 7 sts, 2 hdc in each of next 5 sts, hdc in each of next 7 sts, 2 hdc in next st, join in 2nd ch of beg ch-2, turn. *(29 sts)*

Rnd 3: Ch 1, sc in same st as beg ch-1, 2 sc in next st, sc in each of next 10 sts, 2 sc in each of next 6 sts, sc in each of next 10 sts, 2 sc in next st, join in first sc. *(37 sc)*

Note: *Rnd 3 determines length of the Bootie Sole. If not size required, change hook size and/or yarn weight.*

Upper Foot

Rnd 4: Working in **front lps** (see Stitch Guide), ch 1, sc in same st as beg ch-1, sc in each st around, join in beg sc, turn. (37 sts)

Rnd 5: Ch 2, hdc in each of next 12 sts, [**dc dec** (see Stitch Guide) in next 2 sts] 6 times, hdc in each of next 12 sts, join in 2nd ch of beg ch-2. (31 sts)

Rnd 6: Ch 2, hdc in each of next 9 sts, [dc dec in next 2 sts] 6 times, hdc in each of next 9 sts, join in 2nd ch of beg ch-2. (25 sts)

Rnd 7: Ch 1, sc in same st as beg ch-1, sc in each of next 7 sts, [dc dec in next 2 sts] 5 times, sc in each of next 7 sts, join in beg sc. (20 sts)

Rnd 8: If joining is not at center back of Bootie, sl st in each st to center back, ch 2, dc in each st around, join in 3rd ch of beg ch-3. (20 dc)

Cuff

Rnds 1–3: Ch 2, dc in each st around, join in 2nd ch of beg ch-2. At end of rnd 3, turn.

Rnd 4: Ch 1, sc in same st as beg ch-1, ch 2, [sc in next st, ch 2] around, join in beg sc. Fasten off.

Tie
Make 2.

Cut 2 10-inch lengths of ribbon for Ties. Weave in and out of dc sts of rnd 8. Ties may be anchored by stitching center of each Tie to center back st of rnd 8. Tie ends in a bow. ●

Lacy Reader's Wrap

Design by Elizabeth Ann White

Skill Level
 INTERMEDIATE

Finished Measurements
16 inches wide x 60 inches long

Materials
- Berroco Comfort medium (worsted) weight nylon/acrylic yarn (3½ oz/210 yds/100g per skein):
    4 skeins #9710 ballet pink
- Size I/9/5.5mm crochet hook or size needed to obtain gauge
- Tapestry needle

4 MEDIUM

Gauge
4 shells = 3 inches; 5 shell rows = 2 inches

Pattern Note
Weave in ends as work progresses.

Special Stitch
Shell: (Sc, ch 2, sc) in indicated st or sp.

Wrap
Row 1: Ch 106, **shell** (see Special Stitch) in 2nd ch from hook, [sk next 3 chs, shell in next ch] across, turn. (27 shells)

Row 2: Ch 3, shell in ch-2 sp of each shell across, turn.

Rep row 2 until piece measures 60 inches or desired length. At end of last row, fasten off.

Pocket
Make 2.

Row 1: Ch 29, shell in 2nd ch from hook, [sk next 2 chs, shell in next ch] across, turn. (10 shells)

Rows 2–20: Ch 3, shell in ch-2 sp of each shell across, turn. At end of last row, fasten off.

Finishing
Fold 4 inches of 1 long edge over and tack in place to form collar.

Fold last 5 rows of 1 Pocket over and sew Pocket to Wrap, centered between collar and rem edge as shown in photo.

Fold last 5 rows of last Pocket over and sew Pocket to opposite end of Wrap, centered between collar and rem edge as shown in photo. ●

Banded Slouch Hat

Design by Rebecca Huber

Skill Level

 INTERMEDIATE

Finished Sizes

Instructions given fit woman's size small; changes for medium/large are in [ ].

Finished Measurement

7½ inches *(small)* [8 inches *(medium/large)*] tall

Materials

- Berroco Comfort medium (worsted) weight nylon/acrylic yarn (3½ oz/210 yds/100g per skein):
    - 1 skein each #9703 barley and #9723 rosebud
    - 1 yd #9763 navy blue
- Sizes G/6/4mm and I/9/5.5mm crochet hooks or size needed to obtain gauge
- Tapestry needle
- Stitch marker

Gauge

With size I hook: 8 hdc and 6 rnds = 2 inches

Take time to check gauge.

Pattern Notes

Chain-2 at beginning of round does not count as first half double crochet unless otherwise stated.

Work in continuous rounds; do not turn or join unless otherwise stated.

Mark first stitch of round. Move marker as work progresses.

Join with slip stitch as indicated unless otherwise stated.

Special Stitch

Long single crochet (long sc): Insert hook in indicated st or sp, yo, pull up lp to height of current rnd, yo, pull through all lps on hook.

Hat

Body

Rnd 1: With size I hook and barley, ch 76, taking care not to twist ch, sl st in first ch to form ring, **ch 2** *(see Pattern Notes)*, hdc in each ch around, **place marker** *(see Pattern Notes)*. *(76 sts)*

Rnd 2: Hdc in each st around.

Rep rnd 2 until piece measures 5½ [6] inches long; do not fasten off.

Top

Rnd 1: [Hdc in each of next 6 sts, **hdc dec** *(see Stitch Guide)* in next 2 sts] 9 times, hdc in each rem st around. *(67 sts)*

Rnd 2: [Hdc in each of next 5 sts, hdc dec in next 2 sts] 9 times, hdc in each rem st around. *(58 sts)*

Rnd 3: Hdc in each st around.

Rnd 4: [Hdc in each of next 4 sts, hdc dec in next 2 sts] 9 times, hdc in each rem st around. *(49 sts)*

Rnd 5: [Hdc in each of next 3 sts, hdc dec in next 2 sts] 9 times, hdc in each rem st around. *(40 sts)*

Rnd 6: [Hdc in each of next 2 sts, hdc dec in next 2 sts] 9 times, hdc in each rem st around. *(31 sts)*

Rnd 7: [Hdc in each of next 3 sts, hdc dec in next 2 sts] 6 times, hdc in last st. Leaving long tail, fasten off. *(25 sts)*

Weave tail through sts of last rnd and pull to close top. Secure end with small knot.

Brim

Rnd 1: With RS facing, **join** *(see Pattern Notes)* rosebud in first ch on opposite side of foundation ch, **fpsc** *(see Stitch Guide)* around each hdc on rnd 1 of Body around, **change color** *(see Stitch Guide)* to barley in last st. *(76 sts)*

Size Small Only

Rnd 2: Working in **back lps** *(see Stitch Guide)* behind fpsc of rnd 1, [sc in each of next 17 sts, **sc dec** *(see Stitch Guide)* in next 2 sts] 4 times. *(72 sts)*

Size Medium/Large Only

Rnd [2]: Working in back lps behind fpsc of rnd 1, sc in each st around.

All Sizes

Rnd 3: *Sc in next st, **fpdc** *(see Stitch Guide)* around next st, rep from * around.

Rnds 4–8: Sc in next sc, fpdc around next fpdc, *sc in sp between next sc and next fpdc, fpdc around next fpdc, rep from * around. Change color to rosebud in last st of last rnd.

Rnd 9: *Sc in next sc, ch 1, sk next fpdc, rep from * around. Fasten off.

Emblem

Rnd 1: With size G hook and rosebud, ch 7, change color to barley in last ch, sc in 2nd ch from hook, sc in next ch, hdc in next ch, dc in each of next 2 chs, (3 dc, tr, ch 1, tr, 3 dc) in last ch, working across opposite side of beg ch-7, dc in each of next 2 chs, hdc in next ch, sc in each of last 2 chs.

Rnd 2: Sc in first st, sc in back lp of each of next 7 sts, 2 sc in next st, ch 2, sl st in next ch-1 sp, ch 2, 2 sc in next st, sc in back lp of each of next 7 sts, sc in last st, change color to rosebud.

Rnd 3: Sc in each of next 9 sts, ch 2, **long sc** *(see Special Stitch)* in next st 1 rnd below, (sc, sl st) in next ch-2 sp, 2 long sc in sp between trs on rnd 1, (sc, sl st) in next ch-2 sp, long sc in next st 1 rnd below, ch 2, sc in each of last 9 sts. Fasten off.

Tie triple knot in strand of navy blue. Position knot at base of 2 center long sc made on rnd 3, pull tails through to back of Emblem and secure. Using photo as a guide, sew Emblem to Hat. ●

Shell Stitch Summer Hat

Design by Rebecca Huber

Skill Level

 INTERMEDIATE

Finished Sizes

Instructions given fit woman's size small; changes for medium/large are in [ ].

Finished Measurement

7½ [8] inches tall

Materials

- Berroco Comfort medium (worsted) weight nylon/acrylic yarn (3½ oz/210 yds/100g per skein):
    1 skein each #9705 pretty pink and #9702 pearl
- Size I/9/5.5mm crochet hook or size needed to obtain gauge
- Tapestry needle
- Stitch marker

Gauge

Rnds 1–4 = 2 inches

Take time to check gauge.

Pattern Notes

Work in continuous rounds; do not turn or join unless otherwise stated.

Mark first stitch of round. Move marker as work progresses.

Chain-3 at beginning of round counts as first double crochet and chain-1 unless otherwise stated.

Join with slip stitch as indicated unless otherwise stated.

Special Stitch

Shell: (3 dc, ch 2, 3 dc) as indicated in instructions.

Hat

Rnd 1: With pink, ch 2, 7 sc in first ch, **place marker** (see Pattern Notes). (7 sts)

Rnd 2: 2 sc in each sc around. (14 sts)

Rnd 3: *Sc in next sc, 2 sc in next sc, rep from * around. (21 sts)

Rnd 4: *Sc in each of next 2 sc, 2 sc in next sc, rep from * around. (28 sts)

Rnd 5: *Sc in each of next 3 sc, 2 sc in next sc, rep from * around. (35 sts)

Rnd 6: *Sc in each of next 4 sc, 2 sc in next sc, rep from * around. (42 sts)

Rnd 7: Sc in each sc around.

Rnd 8: *Sc in each of next 5 sc, 2 sc in next sc, rep from * around. (49 sts)

Rnd 9: *Sc in each of next 6 sc, 2 sc in next sc, rep from * around. (56 sts)

Rnd 10: *Sc in each of next 7 sc, 2 sc in next sc, rep from * around. (63 sts)

Rnd 11: *Sc in each of next 8 sc, 2 sc in next sc, rep from * around. (70 sts)

Rnd 12: *Sc in each of next 9 sc, 2 sc in next sc, rep from * around. (77 sts)

Rnd 13: Rep rnd 7.

Size Medium/Large Only

Rnd [14]: *Sc in each of next 10 sc, 2 sc in next sc, rep from * around. ([84] sts)

All Sizes

Rep rnd 7 until Hat measures 4½ [5] inches or desired length from top. **Change color** (see Stitch Guide) to pearl in last st of last rnd.

Next rnd: With pearl, [sc in each of next 24 [20] sc, 2 sc in next sc] 3 [4] times, sc in each rem sc around. Fasten off. (80 [88] sts)

Band

Rnd 1: With pink, sl st in first sc, **ch 3** (see Pattern Notes), *sk next 3 sc, **shell** (see Special Stitch) in next sc, ch 1, sk next 3 sc, dc in next sc, ch 1, rep from * around, **join** (see Pattern Notes) in 2nd ch of beg ch-3. (10 [11] shells, 10 [11] dc)

Rnds 2 & 3: Ch 3, *shell in ch-2 sp of next shell, ch 1**, dc in next dc, ch 1, rep from * around, ending last rep at **, join in 2nd ch of beg ch-3.

Rnd 4: Ch 1, 3 sc in first ch-1 sp, *2 sc in next ch-2 sp, 3 sc in next ch-1 sp, sk next dc**, 3 sc in next ch-1 sp, rep from * around, ending last rep at **, do not fasten off. (80 [88] sc)

Rnd 5: Join pearl in first sc, ch 1, sc in each sc around, change color to pink in last st.

Brim

Rnd 1: With pink, *sc in each of next 2 sc, 2 sc in next sc, rep from * around to last 2 [1] sc, sc in each of last 2 [1] sc. (106 [117] sc)

Rnds 2–6: Sc in each sc around. Fasten off.

Rnd 7: Join pearl in first sc, *sc in next sc, ch 1, sk next sc, sc in next sc, rep from * around. Fasten off. ●

Pigtail Hat

Design by Darla Sims

Skill Level

 INTERMEDIATE

Finished Size

One size fits most

Materials

- Berroco Comfort medium (worsted) weight nylon/acrylic yarn (3½ oz/210 yds/100g per skein):
  - 1 skein each #9705 pretty pink and #9734 liquorice
- Sizes G/6/4mm and I/9/5.5mm crochet hooks or size needed to obtain gauge
- Tapestry needle
- 1½-inch-wide checkered ribbon: 48 inches
- Stitch marker

Gauge

Size I hook: 12 dc = 4 inches

Pattern Note

Weave in loose ends as work progresses.

Work in continuous rounds; do not join or turn unless otherwise stated. Mark first stitch of round.

Join with slip stitch as indicated unless otherwise stated.

Chain-3 at beginning of round counts as a double crochet unless otherwise stated.

Hat

Crown

Rnd 1: With size I hook and pink, ch 2, 8 sc in 2nd ch from hook, **do not join** (see Pattern Notes). (8 sc)

Rnd 2: 2 sc in each st around. (16 sc)

Rnd 3: [Sc in next st, 2 sc in next st] around. (24 sc)

Rnd 4: [Sc in each of next 2 sts, 2 sc in next st] around. (32 sc)

Rnd 5: [Sc in each of next 3 sts, 2 sc in next st] around. (40 sc)

Rnd 6: [Sc in each of next 4 sts, 2 sc in next st] around. (48 sc)

Rnd 7: [Sc in each of next 5 sts, 2 sc in next st] around. *(56 sc)*

Rnd 8: [Sc in each of next 6 sts, 2 sc in next st] around, **join** *(see Pattern Notes)* in beg sc. *(64 sc)*

Side

Rnd 9: Ch 1, sc in same st as beg ch-1, tr in next st, [sc in next st, tr in next st] around, join in beg sc.

Rnds 10 & 11: Ch 3 *(see Pattern Notes)*, dc in each st around, join in 3rd ch of beg ch-3.

Rnd 12: Ch 1, sc in same st as beg ch-1, tr in next st, [sc in next st, tr in next st] around, join in beg sc.

Rnds 13 & 14: Ch 3, dc in each st around, join in 3rd ch of beg ch-3.

Rnd 15: Ch 1, sc in same st as beg ch-1, tr in next st, [sc in next st, tr in next st] around, join in beg sc.

Band

Rnds 1–5: With size G hook, ch 1, sc in each st around, join in beg sc. At end of last rnd, fasten off.

Curly Bangs

With size G hook, join liquorice in any sc, *ch 6, 3 sc in 2nd ch from hook and in each of next 4 chs, sc in next st on Band, sl st in next st, rep from * 5 times, ch 6, 3 sc in 2nd ch from hook and in each of next 4 chs, sc in next st on Band. Fasten off.

Braid
Make 2.

Cut 21 strands liquorice, each 36 inches in length. Holding all strands tog, fold in half and tie knot in center of strands.

Divide strands into 3 groups of 14 strands in each group. Loosely braid groups.

Wrap end of Braid tightly with liquorice. Trim ends.

Cut ribbon in half. Tie 1 piece of ribbon around end of each Braid.

Sew Braids to inside of Band, 2 inches on each side of Curly Bangs. ●

Fantasy Shells Lapghan

Design by Elizabeth Ann White

Skill Level
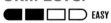 EASY

Finished Measurements
40 inches wide x 41 inches long, excluding Fringe

Gauge
1 shell = 1½ inches; 4 pattern rows = 3½ inches

Pattern Notes
Weave in loose ends as work progresses.

Chain-4 at beginning of row counts as a treble crochet unless otherwise stated.

Materials
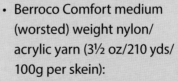

- Berroco Comfort medium (worsted) weight nylon/acrylic yarn (3½ oz/210 yds/100g per skein):
    6 skeins #9780 dried plum
- Size I/9/5.5mm crochet hook or size needed to obtain gauge

Special Stitches

Shell: 5 tr in indicated st or sp.

V-stitch (V-st): (Tr, ch 1, tr) in indicated st or sp.

Lapghan

Row 1: Ch 137, **shell** *(see Special Stitches)* in 5th ch from hook *(beg 4 sk chs count as a tr)*, [sk next 3 chs, **V-st** *(see Special Stitches)* in next ch, sk next 3 chs, shell in next ch] across to last 4 chs, sk next 3 chs, tr in last ch, turn. *(17 shells, 16 V sts, 2 tr)*

Row 2: Ch 4 *(see Pattern Notes)*, V-st in 3rd dc of next shell, [shell in ch-2 sp of next V-st, V-st in 3rd dc of next shell] across to last st, tr in last st, turn.

Row 3: Ch 4, shell in next V-st, [V-st in 3rd dc of next shell, shell in next V-st] across to last st, tr in last st, turn.

Rows 4–49: [Rep rows 2 and 3 alternately] 28 times. At end of last row, fasten off.

Fringe

For each Fringe, cut 6 strands, each 20 inches long. Holding all strands tog, fold in half, insert hook in st or sp, draw fold through st or sp, draw all loose ends through fold, tighten knot. Trim ends.

Place Fringe in first and last st and in sp between each V-st and shell on first and last rows of Lapghan. ●

Glasses Necklace

Design by Sue Childress

Skill Level

 EASY

Finished Measurement

20 inches long

Materials

- Berroco Comfort DK light (DK) weight nylon/acrylic yarn (1¾ oz/178 yds/50g per skein):
    - 1 skein #2722 purple
- Size F/5/3.75mm crochet hook
- Tapestry needle
- Size 3/0 Mill Hill glass beads: 1 package each #05145 pale pink and #05555 new penny

Gauge

Gauge is not important for this project.

Pattern Note

Chain 1 after pulling up bead to secure bead.

Necklace

Getting started: Thread beads on yarn, alternating bead colors.

Row 1: Ch 8, sl st in first ch to form lp, pull up bead, **ch 1** *(see Pattern Note)*, *ch 5, pull up bead, ch 1, rep from * for 27 beads, ch 8, sl st in 8th ch from hook to form lp, turn.

Row 2: *Ch 3**, sc in 3rd ch of next ch-5 sp, pull up bead, ch 1, rep from * across, ending last rep at **, sl st in base of first ch-8 lp. Fasten off. ●

Cuffed Slippers

Design by Marie Griego

Skill Level

 BEGINNER

Finished Sizes

Instructions given fit X-small; changes for small, medium and large are in [ ].

Finished Measurements

Rnd 1 = 5½ inches (x-small) [6¾ inches (small), 8 inches (medium), 9¾ inches (large)]

Materials

- Berroco Comfort medium (worsted) weight nylon/ acrylic yarn (3½ oz/210 yds/ 100g per skein):
  2 skeins #9722 purple
- Size G/6/4mm crochet hook or size needed to obtain gauge
- Tapestry needle
- 3-inch x 6-inch piece of cardboard

Gauge

3 sc = 1 inch

Pattern Notes

Weave in loose ends as work progresses.

Join with slip stitch as indicated unless otherwise stated.

Slipper

Make 2.

Rnd 1: Ch 20 [27, 34, 41], 3 sc in 2nd ch from hook, sc in each ch across to last ch, 3 sc in last ch, working on opposite side of foundation ch, sc in each ch across, **join** (see Pattern Notes) in beg sc. (40 [54, 68, 82] sc)

Rnd 2: Ch 1, sc in same sc as beg ch-1, tr in next sc, [sc in next sc, tr in next sc] around, join in beg sc.

Rnd 3: Ch 1, tr in same sc as beg ch-1, sc in next tr, [tr in next sc, sc in next tr] around, join in beg tr.

Rnd 4: Ch 1, sc in same tr as beg ch-1, tr in next sc, [sc in next tr, tr in next sc] around, join in beg sc.

Rnds 5–10 [5–12, 5–12, 5–12]: [Rep rnds 3 and 4 alternately] 3 [4, 4, 4] times. At end of last rep, leaving 12-inch end, fasten off.

Fold Slipper opening flat across. With tapestry needle and working through both thicknesses, sew across opening to center and secure end.

Cuff
Make 2.

Row 1: Ch 11, sc in 2nd ch from hook, sc in each rem ch across, turn. (10 sc)

Row 2: Ch 1, working in **back lps** (see Stitch Guide), sc in each of next 9 sts, sc through both lps of last sc, turn.

Row 3: Ch 1, working through both lps, sc in first sc, working in back lps, sc in each of next 9 sc, turn.

Rep rows 2 and 3 until beg at center front Cuff is long enough to fit around Slipper opening, ending in same area as beg.

Next row: Beg at center front of opening, holding long edge of Cuff on inside of Slipper opening and working through both thicknesses, sc evenly sp around opening, turn.

Next row: Ch 1, sc evenly sp around entire outer edge of Cuff. Fasten off.

Fold Cuff to outer edge of Slipper.

Pompom
Make 2.

From cardboard, cut 2 circles, each 2½ inches in diameter. Cut a ¾-inch circle from center of each cardboard circle. Holding circles tog, wrap yarn over cardboard circles until filled with yarn. Carefully insert scissors between layers of cardboard, cut strands of yarn around outer edge of circles, place a doubled length of yarn between circles, draw tightly and knot to secure. Remove cardboard circles, fluff Pompom and trim edges as desired. Attach Pompom to center top of Slipper referring to photo. ●

Twilight Flower Throw

Design by Mary Layfield

Skill Level

 INTERMEDIATE

Finished Measurement

48 inches in diameter

Materials

- Berroco Comfort medium (worsted) weight nylon/acrylic yarn (3½ oz/210 yds/100g per skein):
    - 5 skeins #9793 boysenberry heather
    - 1 skein #9794 wild raspberry heather
- Size F/5/3.75mm crochet hook or size needed to obtain gauge
- Tapestry needle

Gauge

Rnds 1–4 = 3¾ inches in diameter

Pattern Notes

Weave in loose ends as work progresses.

Join with slip stitch as indicated unless otherwise stated.

Chain-5 at beginning of round counts as first double crochet and chain-2 space unless otherwise stated.

Chain-3 at beginning of round counts as first double crochet unless otherwise stated.

Special Stitches

Beginning V-stitch (beg V-st): Ch 5 *(see Pattern Notes)*, dc in indicated sp.

V-stitch (V-st): (Dc, ch 2, dc) in indicated sp.

Beginning shell (beg shell): Ch 3 *(see Pattern Notes)*, (dc, ch 2, 2 dc) in indicated sp.

Shell: (2 dc, ch 2, 2 dc) in indicated sp.

Throw

Rnd 1: With wild raspberry heather, ch 8, **join** *(see Pattern Notes)* in first ch to form ring, ch 1, sc in ring, [ch 8, sc in ring] 5 times, ch 4, join with tr in first sc *(counts as ch-8 sp). (6 ch-8 sps)*

Rnd 2: Ch 1, sc in sp formed by joining tr, [ch 8, sc in next ch-8 sp] around, ch 4, join with tr in first sc. *(6 ch-8 sps)*

Rnd 3: Ch 1, (sc, ch 5, sc) in sp formed by joining tr, *ch 5, (sc, ch 5, sc) in next ch-8 sp, rep from * around, ch 2, join with dc in first sc. *(12 ch sps)*

Rnd 4: Ch 1, (sc, ch 5, sc) in sp formed by joining dc, ch 5, *(sc, ch 5, sc) in next ch sp, ch 5, rep from * around, join in beg sc. Fasten off. *(24 ch sps)*

Rnd 5: Join boysenberry heather with sc in any ch sp, [ch 6, sc in next ch sp] around, ch 3, join with dc in first sc. *(24 ch sps)*

Rnd 6: Beg V-st *(see Special Stitches)* in sp formed by joining dc, ch 1, [V-st *(see Special Stitches)* in next ch sp, ch 1] around, join in 3rd ch of beg ch-5. *(24 V-sts, 24 ch sps)*

Rnd 7: Sl st in next ch sp, **beg shell** *(see Special Stitches)*, V-st in ch-2 sp of next V-st, [**shell** *(see Special Stitches)* in ch-2 sp of next V-st, V-st in ch-2 sp of next V-st] around, join in 3rd ch of beg ch-3. *(12 shells, 12 V-sts)*

Rnd 8: Sl st in next st, sl st in next ch-2 sp, beg shell in same sp, ch 1, V-st in ch-2 sp of next V-st, ch 1, [shell in ch-2 sp of next shell, ch 1, V-st in ch-2 sp of next V-st, ch 1] around, join in 3rd ch of beg ch-3. *(24 ch sps, 12 shells, 12 V-sts)*

Rnd 9: Sl st in next st, sl st in next ch-2 sp, beg shell in same sp, ch 2, V-st in next V-st, ch 2, [shell in next shell, ch 2, V-st in next V-st, ch 2] around, join in 3rd ch of beg ch-3.

Rnd 10: Sl st in next st, sl st in next ch-2 sp, beg shell in same sp, ch 3, V-st in next V-st, ch 3, [shell in next shell, ch 3, V-st in next V-st, ch 3] around, join in 3rd ch of beg ch-3.

Rnd 11: Sl st in next st, sl st in next ch sp, beg shell in same sp, ch 4, V-st in next V-st, ch 4, [shell in next shell, ch 4, V-st in next V-st, ch 4] around, join in 3rd ch of beg ch-3.

Rnd 12: Sl st in next st, sl st in next ch-2 sp, beg shell in same sp, ch 5, V-st in next V-st, ch 5, [shell in next shell, ch 5, V-st in next V-st, ch 5] around, join in 3rd ch of beg ch-3.

Rnd 13: Sl st in next st, sl st in next ch sp, beg shell in same sp, ch 3, sc in next ch sp, ch 3, V-st in next V-st, ch 3, sc in next ch sp, ch 3, [shell in next shell, ch 3 sc in next ch sp, ch 3, V-st in next V-st, ch 3, sc in next ch sp, ch 3] around, join in 3rd ch of beg ch-3. *(48 ch sps, 12 shells, 12 V-sts)*

Rnd 14: Sl st in next st, sl st in next ch sp, beg shell in same sp, ch 6, sk next 2 ch sps, V-st in next V-st, ch 6, sk next 2 ch sps, [shell in next shell, ch 5, V-st in next V-st, ch 5] around, join in 3rd ch of beg ch-3. *(24 ch sps, 12 shells, 12 V-sts)*

Rnd 15: Sl st in next st, sl st in next ch sp, beg shell in same sp, ch 4, sc in next ch sp, ch 4, V-st in next V-st, ch 4, sc in next ch sp, ch 4, [shell in next shell, ch 4, sc in next ch sp, ch 4, V-st in next V-st, ch 4, sc in next ch sp, ch 4] around, join in 3rd ch of beg ch-3. *(48 ch sps, 12 shells, 12 V-sts)*

Rnd 16: Sl st in next st, sl st in next ch sp, beg shell in same sp, ch 4, 2 dc in next sc, ch 4, V-st in next V-st, ch 4, 2 dc in next sc, ch 4, [shell in next shell, ch 4, 2 dc in next sc, ch 4, V-st in next V-st, ch 4, 2 dc in next sc, ch 4] around, join in 3rd ch of beg ch-3.

Rnd 17: Sl st in next st, sl st in next ch sp, beg shell in same sp, ch 3, V-st in sp between next 2 dc, ch 3, shell in ch-2 sp of next V-st, ch 3, V-st in sp between next 2 dc, ch 3, [shell in next shell, ch 3, V-st in sp between next 2 dc, ch 3, shell in ch-2 sp of next V-st, ch 3, V-st in sp between next 2 dc, ch 3] around, join in 3rd ch of beg ch-3. *(48 ch sps, 24 shells, 24 V-sts)*

Rnds 18–20: Sl st in next st, sl st in next ch sp, beg shell in same sp, ch 3, V-st in next V-st, ch 3, [shell in next shell, ch 3, V-st in next V-st, ch 3] around, join in 3rd ch of beg ch-3.

Rnd 21: Sl st in next st, sl st in next ch sp, beg shell in same sp, *ch 3, sc in next ch sp, ch 3, V-st in next V-st, ch 3, sc in next ch sp, ch 3**, shell in next shell, rep from * around, ending last rep at **, join in 3rd ch of beg ch-3. *(96 ch sps, 48 shells, 48 V-sts)*

Rnd 22: Sl st in next st, sl st in next ch sp, beg shell in same sp, ch 5, V-st in next V-st, ch 5, [shell in next shell, ch 5, V-st in next V-st, ch 5] around, join in 3rd ch of beg ch-3. *(48 ch sps, 24 shells, 24 V-sts)*

Rnds 23 & 24: Rep rnds 21 and 22.

Rnd 25: Rep rnd 21. At end of rnd, fasten off.

Rnd 26: Join wild raspberry heather in ch-2 sp of first shell, beg shell in same sp, ch 5, shell in ch-2 sp of next V-st, ch 5, [shell in next shell, ch 5, shell in ch-2 sp of next V-st, ch 5] around, join in 3rd ch of beg ch-3. *(48 ch sps, 48 shells)*

Rnd 27: Sl st in next st, sl st in next ch sp, beg shell in same sp, ch 4, sc in next ch sp, ch 4, [shell in next shell, ch 4, sc in next ch sp, ch 4] around, join in 3rd ch of beg ch-3. *(96 ch sps, 48 shells)*

Rnd 28: Sl st in next st, sl st in next ch sp, beg shell in same sp, ch 6, [shell in next shell, ch 6] around, join in 3rd ch of beg ch-3. Fasten off. *(48 shells, 48 ch sps)*

Rnd 29: Join boysenberry heather in ch-2 sp of first shell, beg shell in same sp, ch 4, sc in next ch sp, ch 4, [shell in next shell, ch 4, sc in next ch sp, ch 4] around, join in 3rd ch of beg ch-3. *(96 ch sps, 48 shells)*

Rnd 30: Sl st in next st, sl st in next ch sp, beg shell in same sp, ch 7, [shell in next shell, ch 7] around, join in 3rd ch of beg ch-3. Fasten off. *(48 shells, 48 ch sps)*

Rnd 31: Sl st in next st, sl st in next ch sp, beg shell in same sp, ch 4, sc in next ch sp, ch 4, [shell in next shell, ch 4, sc in next ch sp, ch 4] around, join in 3rd ch of beg ch-3. *(96 ch sps, 48 shells)*

Rnd 32: Sl st in next st, sl st in next ch sp, beg shell in same sp, ch 4, dc in next sc, ch 4, [shell in next shell, ch 4, dc in next sc, ch 4] around, join in 3rd ch of beg ch-3. *(96 ch sps, 48 shells, 48 dc)*

Rnd 33: Sl st in next st, sl st in next ch sp, beg shell in same sp, ch 4, 2 dc in next dc, ch 4, [shell in next shell, ch 4, 2 dc in next dc, ch 4] around, join in 3rd ch of beg ch-3. *(96 ch sps, 96 dc, 48 shells)*

Rnd 34: Sl st in next st, sl st in next ch sp, beg shell in same sp, ch 4, 3 dc in sp between next 2 dc, ch 4, [shell in next shell, ch 4, 3 dc in sp between next 2 dc, ch 4] around, join in 3rd ch of beg ch-3. *(144 dc, 96 ch sps, 48 shells)*

Rnd 35: Sl st in next st, sl st in next ch sp, beg shell in same sp, ch 4, 4 dc in center st of next 3-dc group, ch 4, [shell in next shell, ch 4, 4 dc in center st of next 3-dc group, ch 4] around, join in 3rd ch of beg ch-3. *(192 dc, 96 ch sps, 48 shells)*

Rnds 36–38: Sl st in next st, sl st in next ch sp, beg shell in same sp, ch 3, 4 dc in sp between 2nd and 3rd sts of next 4-dc group, ch 3, [shell in next shell, ch 3, 4 dc in between 2nd and 3rd sts of next 4-dc group, ch 3] around, join in 3rd ch of beg ch-3. *(96 ch sps, 48 4-dc groups, 48 shells)*

Rnd 39: Sl st in next st, sl st in next ch sp, beg shell in same sp, ch 3, (dc, ch 3, dc) in sp between 2nd and 3rd sts of next 4-dc group, ch 3, [shell in next shell, ch 3, (dc, ch 3, dc) in sp between 2nd and 3rd sts of next 4-dc group, ch 3] around, join in 3rd ch of beg ch-3. *(144 ch sps, 96 dc, 48 shells)*

Rnd 40: Sl st in next st, sl st in next ch sp, beg shell in same sp, ch 3, sk next ch sp, (dc, {ch 3, dc} twice) in next ch sp, ch 3, sk next ch sp, [shell in next shell, ch 3, sk next ch sp, (dc, {ch 3, dc} twice) in next ch sp, ch 3, sk next ch sp] around, join in 3rd ch of beg ch-3. *(192 ch sps, 144 dc, 48 shells)*

Rnd 41: Sl st in next st, sl st in next ch sp, beg shell in same sp, ch 2, sk next ch sp, (dc, ch 3, dc) in each of next 2 ch sps, ch 2, sk next ch sp, [shell in next shell, ch 2, sk next ch sp, (dc, ch 3, dc) in each of next 2 ch sps, ch 2, sk next ch sp] around, join in 3rd ch of beg ch-3. *(192 dc, 192 ch sps, 48 shells)*

Rnd 42: Sl st in next st, sl st in next ch sp, beg shell in same sp, *ch 2, sk next ch sp, (dc, ch 3, dc) in next ch sp, dc in sp between next 2 dc, (dc, ch 3, dc) in next ch sp, ch 2, sk next ch sp**, shell in next shell, rep from * around, ending last rep at **, join in 3rd ch of beg ch-3. *(240 dc, 192 ch sps, 48 shells)*

Rnds 43–48: Sl st in next st, sl st in next ch sp, beg shell in same sp, *ch 2, sk next ch sp, (dc, ch 3, dc) in next ch sp, sk next dc, dc in next dc, (dc, ch 3, dc) in next ch sp, ch 2, sk next ch sp**, shell in next shell, rep from * around, ending last rep at **, join in 3rd ch of beg ch-3. At end of last row, fasten off.

Rnd 49: Join wild raspberry heather in ch-2 sp of first shell, beg shell in same sp, *ch 2, sk next ch sp, (dc, ch 3, dc) in next ch sp, sk next dc, dc in next dc, (dc, ch 3, dc) in next ch sp, ch 2, sk next ch sp**, shell in next shell, rep from * around, ending last rep at **, join in 3rd ch of beg ch-3. Fasten off.

Trim

Join wild raspberry heather with sc in ch-2 sp of any shell on rnd 49, ch 4, sc in same sp, *ch 4, sc in next ch sp on rnd 49, ch 4, sc in next ch sp on rnd before last between next 2 dc on last rnd, [ch 4, sc in corresponding sp on rnd below] 9 times, ch 4, sc in sp between 2nd and 3rd dc of 4-dc group on rnd below, ch 4, sk next dc on rnd above, sc in next ch sp, [ch 4, sc in corresponding sp on rnd above] 9 times, ch 4, sc in next sp on rnd 49 above, ch 4**, (sc, ch 4, sc) in ch-2 sp of next shell, rep from * around, ending last rep at **, join in beg sc. Fasten off. ●

STITCH GUIDE

Need help? ▶ **StitchGuide.com** • ILLUSTRATED GUIDES • HOW-TO VIDEOS

STITCH ABBREVIATIONS

beg	begin/begins/beginning
bpdc	back post double crochet
bpsc	back post single crochet
bptr	back post treble crochet
CC	contrasting color
ch(s)	chain(s)
ch-	refers to chain or space previously made (i.e., ch-1 space)
ch sp(s)	chain space(s)
cl(s)	cluster(s)
cm	centimeter(s)
dc	double crochet (singular/plural)
dc dec	double crochet 2 or more stitches together, as indicated
dec	decrease/decreases/decreasing
dtr	double treble crochet
ext	extended
fpdc	front post double crochet
fpsc	front post single crochet
fptr	front post treble crochet
g	gram(s)
hdc	half double crochet
hdc dec	half double crochet 2 or more stitches together, as indicated
inc	increase/increases/increasing
lp(s)	loop(s)
MC	main color
mm	millimeter(s)
oz	ounce(s)
pc	popcorn(s)
rem	remain/remains/remaining
rep(s)	repeat(s)
rnd(s)	round(s)
RS	right side
sc	single crochet (singular/plural)
sc dec	single crochet 2 or more stitches together, as indicated
sk	skip/skipped/skipping
sl st(s)	slip stitch(es)
sp(s)	space(s)/spaced
st(s)	stitch(es)
tog	together
tr	treble crochet
trtr	triple treble
WS	wrong side
yd(s)	yard(s)
yo	yarn over

YARN CONVERSION

OUNCES TO GRAMS		GRAMS TO OUNCES	
1	28.4	25	⅞
2	56.7	40	1⅔
3	85.0	50	1¾
4	113.4	100	3½

UNITED STATES		UNITED KINGDOM
sl st (slip stitch)	=	sc (single crochet)
sc (single crochet)	=	dc (double crochet)
hdc (half double crochet)	=	htr (half treble crochet)
dc (double crochet)	=	tr (treble crochet)
tr (treble crochet)	=	dtr (double treble crochet)
dtr (double treble crochet)	=	ttr (triple treble crochet)
skip	=	miss

Single crochet decrease (sc dec): (Insert hook, yo, draw lp through) in each of the sts indicated, yo, draw through all lps on hook.

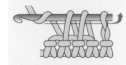

Example of 2-sc dec

Half double crochet decrease (hdc dec): (Yo, insert hook, yo, draw lp through) in each of the sts indicated, yo, draw through all lps on hook.

Example of 2-hdc dec

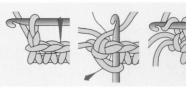

Reverse single crochet (reverse sc): Ch 1, sk first st, working from left to right, insert hook in next st from front to back, draw up lp on hook, yo and draw through both lps on hook.

Chain (ch): Yo, pull through lp on hook.

Single crochet (sc): Insert hook in st, yo, pull through st, yo, pull through both lps on hook.

Double crochet (dc): Yo, insert hook in st, yo, pull through st, [yo, pull through 2 lps] twice.

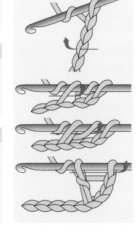

Double crochet decrease (dc dec): (Yo, insert hook, yo, draw lp through, yo, draw through 2 lps on hook) in each of the sts indicated, yo, draw through all lps on hook.

Example of 2-dc dec

Front loop (front lp) Back loop (back lp)

Front Loop   Back Loop

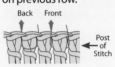

Front post stitch (fp): Back post stitch (bp): When working post st, insert hook from right to left around post of st on previous row.

Back   Front

Post of Stitch

Half double crochet (hdc): Yo, insert hook in st, yo, pull through st, yo, pull through all 3 lps on hook.

Double treble crochet (dtr): Yo 3 times, insert hook in st, yo, pull through st, [yo, pull through 2 lps] 4 times.

Treble crochet decrease (tr dec): Holding back last lp of each st, tr in each of the sts indicated, yo, pull through all lps on hook.

Example of 2-tr dec

Slip stitch (sl st): Insert hook in st, pull through both lps on hook.

Chain color change (ch color change) Yo with new color, draw through last lp on hook.

Double crochet color change (dc color change) Drop first color, yo with new color, draw through last 2 lps of st.

Treble crochet (tr): Yo twice, insert hook in st, yo, pull through st, [yo, pull through 2 lps] 3 times.

Metric Conversion Charts

METRIC CONVERSIONS				
yards	x	.9144	=	metres (m)
yards	x	91.44	=	centimetres (cm)
inches	x	2.54	=	centimetres (cm)
inches	x	25.40	=	millimetres (mm)
inches	x	.0254	=	metres (m)

centimetres	x	.3937	=	inches
metres	x	1.0936	=	yards

INCHES INTO MILLIMETRES & CENTIMETRES (Rounded off slightly)

inches	mm	cm	inches	cm	inches	cm	inches	cm
1/8	3	0.3	5	12.5	21	53.5	38	96.5
1/4	6	0.6	5 1/2	14	22	56	39	99
3/8	10	1	6	15	23	58.5	40	101.5
1/2	13	1.3	7	18	24	61	41	104
5/8	15	1.5	8	20.5	25	63.5	42	106.5
3/4	20	2	9	23	26	66	43	109
7/8	22	2.2	10	25.5	27	68.5	44	112
1	25	2.5	11	28	28	71	45	114.5
1 1/4	32	3.2	12	30.5	29	73.5	46	117
1 1/2	38	3.8	13	33	30	76	47	119.5
1 3/4	45	4.5	14	35.5	31	79	48	122
2	50	5	15	38	32	81.5	49	124.5
2 1/2	65	6.5	16	40.5	33	84	50	127
3	75	7.5	17	43	34	86.5		
3 1/2	90	9	18	46	35	89		
4	100	10	19	48.5	36	91.5		
4 1/2	115	11.5	20	51	37	94		

KNITTING NEEDLES CONVERSION CHART

Canada/U.S.	0	1	2	3	4	5	6	7	8	9	10	10½	11	13	15
Metric (mm)	2	2¼	2¾	3¼	3½	3¾	4	4½	5	5½	6	6½	8	9	10

CROCHET HOOKS CONVERSION CHART

Canada/U.S.	1/B	2/C	3/D	4/E	5/F	6/G	8/H	9/I	10/J	10½/K	N
Metric (mm)	2.25	2.75	3.25	3.5	3.75	4.25	5	5.5	6	6.5	9.0

Annie's® *Caring Crochet* is published by Annie's, 306 East Parr Road, Berne, IN 46711. Printed in USA. Copyright ©2015, 2017 Annie's. All rights reserved. This publication may not be reproduced in part or in whole without written permission from the publisher.

RETAIL STORES: If you would like to carry this publication or any other Annie's publication, visit AnniesWSL.com.

Every effort has been made to ensure that the instructions in this publication are complete and accurate. We cannot, however, take responsibility for human error, typographical mistakes or variations in individual work. Please visit AnniesCustomerService.com to check for pattern updates.

ISBN: 978-1-57367-770-7

3 4 5 6 7 8 9